cooking with
BOURBON
&BEER

ISBN-13: 978-1-56383-483-7
Item #7115

**Printed in the USA
by G&R Publishing Co.**

Distributed By:

CQProducts

507 Industrial Street
Waverly, IA 50677

www.cqbookstore.com

gifts@cqbookstore.com

CQ Products

CQ Products

@cqproducts

@cqproducts

BOURBON

*Take your favorite drinks from the bar to the kitchen for **bourbon tastin'**, **beer sippin'**, **great eatin'** recipes.*

Why?

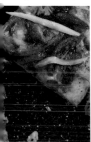

1 You already love bourbon and beer, so why not add them to your food?

2 Flavor, flavor, flavor!

3 Bourbon & beer play well together *(but each is perfectly capable of carrying a spirited dish on its own, too).*

4 Nothing beats beer batters for frying everything from pickles to fish.

5 Bourbon-laced glazes add flavor to wings, salmon, caramel corn, kabobs and so much more.

6 Breads, cheese spreads, soups, and sandwiches just taste better with a little booze tucked inside.

7 A bite of this, a sip of that makes you and your friends very happy!

The proof is in the tasting!

& BEER

FLATBREAD APPETIZERS

2 T. unsalted butter

¼ C. olive oil, divided

2 sweet white onions, sliced

Salt

Sugar

1 C. **porter beer**

2 (6.5 oz.) pkgs pizza crust mix

½ tsp. garlic salt

1 C. **malty beer**

2¼ C. shredded smoked Gouda cheese

1½ C. grape or cherry tomatoes, sliced

½ tsp. black pepper

2 T. fresh parsley, chopped

Melt together the butter and 2 tablespoons oil in a big saucepan over medium-low heat. Add the onions and a pinch of both salt and sugar; cover and cook 10 to 15 minutes, until softened. Stir in the porter and cook until nearly evaporated and the mixture becomes glaze-like, all the while sipping the leftover porter and stirring the onions.

Preheat the oven to 400° and cover two rimmed baking sheets with parchment paper. In a big bowl, combine the crust mix and garlic salt. Microwave the malty beer on high for 20 seconds or until warmed to 110°; pour into the bowl, stirring until dough forms. Cover and let stand 5 minutes.

Divide the dough into six equal pieces; flour lightly and press each into a 6" circle on the prepped baking sheets. Prebake the crusts about 3 minutes. Top with the Gouda and caramelized onions. In a bowl, mix the tomatoes with the remaining 2 tablespoons oil, black pepper, and a little salt; divide among the crusts. Brush exposed dough with any oil remaining in the bowl. Bake for 15 to 20 minutes, until the crusts have turned a light golden brown. Sprinkle with parsley and cut into appetizer-size servings.

Bourbon

COCKTAIL-INSPIRED PECANS

¼ C. dried cherries
¼ C. **bourbon**
2 T. brown sugar
1 tsp. salt
¼ tsp. black pepper

¼ tsp. cayenne pepper
2 C. pecan halves
2 T. unsalted butter
1 T. orange zest

Soak the dried cherries in the bourbon for at least 1 hour.

In a small bowl, stir together the brown sugar, salt, black pepper, and cayenne. Line a rimmed baking sheet with parchment paper. Set these things aside.

To toast the pecans, put them in a single layer in a big non-stick skillet over medium heat about 8 minutes or until they just start to look a little toasty, stirring often. Drop the butter into the hot skillet with the toasted pecans, letting it melt; stir to fully coat the pecans. Sprinkle the set-aside sugar mixture evenly over the pecans and stir again to coat. Take the skillet off the heat and stir in the cherries and the bourbon they were soaking in.

Return the pan to the heat for a few minutes, until the liquid is absorbed and the pecans are nicely glazed. Spread evenly on the prepped baking sheet and let 'em cool.

Once the pecans are cool to the touch, sprinkle with the zest.

Grab a few. Grab a few more. Realize they're habit-forming. Make more.

Bourbon

Ice Cream Manhattan

Chill 2 large glasses. Beat ½ C. heavy cream until frothy; add 2¼ tsp. sweet vermouth, 1½ tsp. sugar, and a dash of Angostura bitters and beat until soft peaks form. Chill. Place 2 or 3 scoops of vanilla ice cream into the chilled glasses and add ¾ oz. (1½ T.) **bourbon** *and 1 T. maraschino cherry juice to each. Fill with cold cherry soda and top with the prepped whipped cream and a cherry.* **serves 2**

MAKES 7 CUPS

CARAMEL CORN WITH BOURBONALITY

Preheat the oven to 300°. Line a rimmed baking sheet with parchment paper and dig out a rubber spatula. Dump 6 C. popped popcorn into a big bowl and add a handful of salted peanuts. In a medium saucepan over medium heat, combine 6 T. butter, ⅓ C. dark brown sugar, 3 T. light corn syrup, and a heaping ¼ tsp. salt until it comes to a boil, stirring often. Boil 5 minutes, stirring constantly. Take the pan off the heat and stir in 1 tsp. vanilla and ¼ C. **bourbon**; pour over the popcorn and stir to coat. Spread out over the prepped baking sheet and sprinkle with a little extra salt if you'd like. Bake for 35 minutes, stirring once. Remove from the oven and let stand 15 minutes. Seriously addicting.

Beer

BEERBQ PARTY MEATBALLS

Preheat the oven to 375° and line a couple of rimmed baking sheets with foil; coat with cooking spray and set aside.

Dump 1 C. panko bread crumbs into a big bowl and add 2 lbs. lean ground beef, 1½ tsp. minced garlic, 2 beaten eggs, 1 T. Worcestershire sauce, 1 tsp. black pepper, and 2 tsp. salt. Get in there with your hands and mix it up. Use a level measuring tablespoon to form the meatballs, roll them in your hands to round them out, and then arrange them in the prepped pans.

In a bowl, whisk together 1 C. BBQ sauce, 1 C. **beer** *(we used lager)*, 1 tsp. Sriracha sauce, and ½ tsp. salt. Pour this evenly over the meatballs and bake 40 to 45 minutes.

SERVES 4

SLOW & EASY STEAK & ALE SOUP

2 T. olive oil, divided

¼ C. flour

½ tsp. each salt & black pepper

1 lb. chuck roast, trimmed & cut into bite-size pieces

1 onion, sliced

1 to 2 C. sliced mushrooms

1 celery rib, sliced

1 T. minced garlic

2 large potatoes, cut into bite-size pieces

1 (12 oz.) bottle **beer** *(we used extra pale ale)*, plus more for thinning

1 chicken bouillon cube

½ tsp. dried thyme

1 (5 oz.) can evaporated milk

1½ C. shredded sharp cheddar cheese

Heat 1 tablespoon of the oil in a skillet over medium heat. Mix the flour, salt, and black pepper in a big zippered plastic bag. Toss in the cubed meat and shake to coat. Put the coated cubes in the hot oil and cook until browned on all sides, turning as needed. Transfer the browned meat to a 3-quart slow cooker.

Return the skillet to the heat and add the remaining 1 tablespoon oil. Add the onion, mushrooms, celery, and garlic and cook until the onions are crisp-tender; dump into the slow cooker along with the potatoes. Add the beer, bouillon cube, and thyme. Cover and cook on high 3½ hours or until thickened and potatoes are tender.

Turn off the cooker and pour in the evaporated milk. Stir in the cheese, cover, and let set for 10 minutes or until the cheese is melted. Stir again before serving. For a thinner soup, stir in water or a little extra beer.

Garlic & Herb Beer Bread

Grease a 5 x 9" loaf pan with cooking spray and melt ¼ C. butter in the microwave; set both aside. In a big bowl, mix 2 C. whole wheat flour, 1 C. all-purpose flour, 3 T. sugar, 1 T. baking powder, and 1 tsp. each garlic powder, salt, dried rosemary, dried thyme, and dried oregano. Stir in 12 oz. of your favorite **beer** *(we used extra pale ale)* until just mixed. Coat the bottom of the prepped pan with 2 T. of the melted butter. Spread the batter in the pan and brush the remaining 2 T. butter over the top. Bake for 50 minutes or until the bread tests done. ***makes 1 loaf***

SERVES 12

BOURBONATED CHEESECAKE

¼ C. melted unsalted butter, cooled

¾ C. graham cracker crumbs

½ C. finely chopped pecans

¾ C. brown sugar, divided

¾ C. plus 3½ T. sugar, divided

1½ C. pumpkin puree

3 eggs

1 tsp. vanilla

2 T. plus ¾ C. heavy cream, divided

3 T. plus 2 tsp. **bourbon**, divided

1 T. cornstarch

2½ tsp. cinnamon

1 tsp. each ground nutmeg and ginger

¼ tsp. ground cloves

½ tsp. salt

3 (8 oz.) pkgs. cream cheese, softened

2 C. sour cream

Pecan halves, optional

Mix butter, crumbs, pecans, and ¼ cup each brown sugar and sugar; press firmly onto the bottom and ½" up the sides of a greased 9" springform pan. Chill 1 hour.

Preheat the oven to 350°. Whisk together the pumpkin, eggs, vanilla, 2 tablespoons cream, and 2 tablespoons bourbon; set aside. In a big mixing bowl, mix the cornstarch, cinnamon, nutmeg, ginger, cloves, salt, ½ cup sugar, and the remaining ½ cup brown sugar. Add the cream cheese and beat until smooth. Add the set-aside pumpkin mixture and beat until combined. Pour the filling into the chilled crust and smooth the top. Set on a rimmed baking sheet and place in the oven. Bake for 50 to 60 minutes or until just set. Remove pans from the oven and set on a cooling rack for 5 minutes. Don't turn off the oven.

Mix the sour cream, 2 tablespoons sugar, and 1 tablespoon bourbon until smooth; spread evenly over the cheesecake. Return pans to oven and bake 3 minutes. Turn off oven, but leave the cheesecake inside for 3 hours or until cool. Cover and chill for 4 hours before removing the sides of the pan.

Beat together the remaining ¾ cup cream, 1½ tablespoons sugar, and 2 teaspoons bourbon until stiff peaks form; use to frost cheesecake as desired. Garnish with pecan halves.

Bourbon

Freezer Slush

*In a freezer container, mix 5½ C. water, 3½ C. pineapple juice, 1 C. sugar, 1 (12 oz.) can frozen lemonade concentrate, ½ (12 oz.) can frozen orange juice concentrate, 2 tsp. instant tea mix, and 8 oz. (1 C.) **bourbon**. Stir, cover, and freeze. Take it straight from the freezer and shave into a glass, or thaw in the refrigerator for your slushy drinking pleasure. If you want it fizzy, stir in lemon-lime soda. **makes about 12 cups***

SPIKED POPPYSEED MUFFINS

2½ C. flour

1¾ tsp. baking powder

¼ tsp. baking soda

1 tsp. coarse salt

2 eggs, room temperature

1 C. plus 2½ T. sugar, divided

1½ tsp. lemon zest, plus more for sprinkling

Juice of 2 medium lemons, divided

¼ C. plus ⅓ C. **beer**, room temperature *(we used Boston Lager)*

½ C. unsalted butter, melted & cooled

2 to 3 T. poppy seed

Coarse sugar for sprinkling, optional

Powdered sugar

Preheat the oven to 350°. Grease 12 muffin cups and set aside. In a big bowl, mix the flour, baking powder, baking soda, and salt. In a separate bowl, whisk together the eggs, 1 cup sugar, 1½ teaspoons zest, and ¼ cup each lemon juice and beer. Whisk in the butter until blended, then stir this mixture into the dry ingredients until just combined. Stir in the poppy seed and divide evenly among the prepped muffin cups; sprinkle with coarse sugar for extra texture if you'd like. Bake 18 to 20 minutes, until muffins test done. Set the pan on a cooling rack for 5 minutes before removing the muffins.

In the meantime, whisk together the remaining ⅓ cup beer, 2½ tablespoons sugar, and 1 teaspoon lemon juice. With a toothpick or skewer, pierce the top of each warm muffin several times and slowly pour some of the beer mixture over each one, letting it soak leisurely into the holes.

Whisk together about 1 tablespoon lemon juice with enough powdered sugar to make a drizzling consistency. Drizzle over muffins and sprinkle with more zest. Lick the bowl.

Irish Beef Stew

Heat 2 T. olive oil in a saucepan over medium-high heat; add 1½ lbs. stew meat *(cut into ½" pieces)* and 1 chopped onion. Cook for 8 minutes, stirring occasionally. Pour in 1 (12 oz.) bottle **stout beer** and 1¼ C. tomato sauce; bring to a boil. Add 2 tsp. chopped fresh rosemary, reduce the heat, cover, and simmer for 2 hours or until the meat is tender. Stir in 1 C. frozen peas, season with salt and pepper, and ladle into bowls. *serves 3*

SERVES A CROWD

BEER & PRETZEL CHEESE BALL

2 (8 oz.) pkgs. cream cheese, softened

2 C. finely shredded Mexican cheese blend

1 (1 oz.) pkg. dry ranch dip mix

⅓ C. **beer** *(we used pretzel wheat ale)*

5 bacon strips, cooked & crumbled

1 (2 oz.) jar pimentos *(drained)*

3 green onions, *sliced*

½ C. crushed pretzels

Pretzels for serving

Beat cream cheese in a mixing bowl on medium speed until light and fluffy. Beat in Mexican cheese blend and dip mix. Slowly pour in beer and continue mixing until well blended. Stir in the bacon, pimentos, and green onions.

Line a small bowl with plastic wrap, letting the ends hang over the edges; pack in the cheese mixture so it takes the shape of the bowl, flattening the top. Wrap the ends of the plastic over the cheese and set in the fridge for several hours.

When it's chilled, remove the cheese from the bowl and take off the plastic. Press the crushed pretzels all over the sides of the cheese ball. Serve with pretzels.

WHY DO BEER AND PRETZELS TASTE SO GOOD TOGETHER? WHO KNOWS! BUT IT'S TRUE, AND THIS CHEESE BALL HELPS CURB THAT CRAVING BY INCLUDING BOTH!

Beer-garitas

*Mix 2 (16 oz.) cans chilled **beer** (we used light beer), 1 C. tequila, and 1 (12 oz.) can frozen limeade concentrate (thawed) in a big pitcher. Rim five glasses with lime juice and salt, fill glasses with ice, and pour in the margarita mixture. Garnish with lime wedges. Fantastic!*

Bourbon

SERVES 6

SURPRISE CHILI

2 lbs. lean ground beef

1 T. olive oil

1 red onion, chopped

2 bell peppers, any color, chopped

1 (28 oz.) can petite diced tomatoes

2½ tsp. minced garlic

3 to 4 T. chili powder

½ tsp. cayenne pepper

1 tsp. paprika

2 to 3 tsp. ground cumin

Salt & black pepper to taste

2 oz. dark chocolate

¼ to ½ C. **bourbon**

Sour cream, shredded cheddar cheese, corn chips, and cooked bacon

In your favorite big saucepan, brown the ground beef in hot oil over medium heat. After a few minutes, toss in the onion and peppers. Let that cook until the veggies have softened and the meat is cooked through. Drain if you'd like.

Stir in the tomatoes, garlic, chili powder, cayenne, paprika, cumin, salt, and black pepper; bring to a boil, reduce heat, cover, and simmer for 1 hour, stirring occasionally. If you want a thinner chili, go ahead and stir in some water.

Break the chocolate into small pieces and toss it into the chili, stirring until melted. Now stir in the bourbon. Take a whiff! It smells amazing!

Top each bowl of chili with sour cream, cheese, chips, and bacon. It's sooo good!

DARK CHOCOLATE: A TASTY LITTLE SURPRISE FOR CHILI.

Skillet Bourbon Cornbread

Preheat the oven to 350° and grease a 12" cast iron skillet. In a medium bowl, stir together 2 C. white flour, 1 C. each whole wheat flour, sugar, and cornmeal, 2 T. baking powder, and 1½ tsp. salt. In a separate bowl, whisk together ½ C. **bourbon**, 1 C. buttermilk, 1 C. melted & cooled butter, and 2 beaten eggs; pour into the dry ingredients and stir until just combined. Transfer to the skillet and sprinkle with coarse ground black pepper. Bake for 25 to 30 minutes or until it tests done. Yummer! *serves 12*

CHOCOLATE PORTER PIE

1 (4 oz.) pkg. semi-sweet baking chocolate

2½ T. plus ¼ C. **chocolate porter beer**, divided

1½ T. plus 3¾ C. heavy cream, divided

1 purchased 9" chocolate pie crust

1 (4 oz.) pkg. unsweetened baking chocolate

1¼ C. powdered sugar, divided

8 oz. mascarpone cheese, softened

1 tsp. vanilla

Chop the semi-sweet chocolate and toss into a small bowl. Microwave 2½ tablespoons beer with 1½ tablespoons cream until it's just starting to steam; pour over the chocolate, let stand to soften, and stir until melted. Pour into the crust and chill for ½ hour.

Chop the unsweetened chocolate and put into the same bowl. Combine ¼ cup cream and the remaining ¼ cup beer and microwave until steaming; pour over the chocolate, let stand to soften, and stir until melted. Let it hang out until it has cooled to room temperature.

In a chilled mixing bowl, beat 1½ cups cream with ½ cup powdered sugar on high speed until soft peaks form. With the mixer running, slowly add the cooled chocolate mixture, beating until stiff peaks form; spread over the chocolate layer in the pie plate. Chill until set. The rest of the porter? You get to drink it!

Beat the mascarpone and remaining ¾ cup powdered sugar. Add the vanilla and remaining 2 cups cream, beating until medium peaks form. Mound on top of the pie and chill.

SERVES 4

CHOPS WITH MUSHROOM-BOURBON CREAM

5 T. grapeseed oil, divided

1 lb. white mushrooms, sliced

¼ C. chopped onion

2 big garlic cloves, chopped

½ C. dry white wine (like Sauvignon Blanc)

1 C. chicken stock

¼ C. plus 2 T. **bourbon**, divided

½ C. heavy cream

About ⅓ C. flour

1 egg

1½ C. fresh bread crumbs

4 (6 to 7 oz.) center cut pork chops

Salt & black pepper to taste

2 T. finely chopped fresh basil

Heat 2 tablespoons oil in a big skillet over medium-high heat and add the mushrooms, onion, and garlic; sauté 10 minutes or until the mushrooms have browned. Add the wine and bring to a boil; boil several minutes, until the liquid is reduced to a glaze-like consistency. Add the stock and ¼ cup bourbon and boil until reduced by about ⅔. Stir in the cream and simmer until the sauce thickens. Congratulations! You have just created delicious Bourbon Cream; just set it aside for now.

Put flour into a shallow bowl. In a separate shallow bowl, whisk the egg with the remaining 2 tablespoons bourbon, and put the bread crumbs into yet another bowl. Sprinkle both sides of the pork with salt and black pepper; dip into the flour, then the egg, and then the bread crumbs so the chops are completely coated.

Heat the remaining 3 tablespoons oil in a separate big skillet over medium-high heat. Add the coated chops and fry 4 minutes per side, until browned. Flip the chops again, reduce the heat to low, cover, and cook for 5 minutes or until done.

Reheat the Bourbon Cream, stir in the basil and more salt and pepper, and serve the chops with the sauce for flavor that is just incredible!

Hop, Ship & Go Naked

*In a shaker, combine 1 oz. (2 T.) **bourbon**, 1½ T. fresh lemon juice, and 1½ T. grenadine syrup; shake vigorously. Pour into a tall glass filled with ice and fill to the top with 6 to 8 oz. of your favorite chilled **beer** (we used lager). **serves 1***

SERVES 4

INEBRIATED STOUT-GLAZED POLLOCK

2 (12 oz.) bottles
stout beer

⅓ C. honey

1 T. lemon juice

½ tsp. hot sauce

½ tsp. salt

1 (16 oz.) pkg. frozen
pollock fillets, thawed
& patted dry

Olive oil

Coarse black pepper

4 large carrots, cut into
½"-thick sticks

Let's get this fish inebriated! In a medium skillet, bring the beer and honey to a boil over medium heat; skim foam off the top. Simmer about 45 minutes or until it's reduced to about ¾ cup glaze; transfer to a bowl and stir in lemon juice, hot sauce, and salt. Set aside until cool.

Pour ½ cup of the cooled glaze over the fish in a shallow baking dish; turn to coat. Cover and refrigerate several hours. Set the remaining glaze aside.

Preheat the broiler. Remove the fish from the marinade and arrange on a greased broiler pan. Brush with oil and season with black pepper. Broil 4" from the heat for 4 to 5 minutes or until cooked through.

In the meantime, cook the carrots until crisp-tender; serve the carrots with the fish, brushing the fish *(and the carrots if you'd like)* with the set-aside glaze.

Orange-Ale Vinaigrette

In a blender, process ¼ C. plus 2 T. **beer** *(we used India pale ale)*, 1 T. finely chopped shallot, 1 tsp. orange zest, 1 T. plus 1 tsp. honey, and 1 tsp. Dijon mustard until combined. With the motor running, gradually add ¼ C. olive oil in a thin stream until well mixed. Season with salt and pepper and serve over mixed greens. Delicious! *makes ½ cup*

BOURBON'S BACON ME CRAZY MAC & CHEESE

½ C. plus 1 T. **bourbon**, divided

¾ C. brown sugar

1 tsp. cayenne pepper

10 bacon strips

1 lb. uncooked large elbow macaroni

3 T. unsalted butter

⅓ C. flour

2 C. milk

3 C. shredded sharp cheddar cheese

1 C. shredded provolone cheese

½ tsp. paprika

Salt & black pepper to taste

Preheat the oven to 400° and line a rimmed baking sheet with foil; coat the foil with cooking spray and set aside.

Bring ½ cup bourbon to a boil in a small saucepan. Reduce the heat and simmer until reduced to just 2 or 3 tablespoons. Mix the brown sugar and cayenne on a plate and dredge both sides of the bacon in it, pressing well to adhere; arrange on the prepped baking sheet and bake for 7 minutes; flip and bake 5 minutes more or until almost crisp. Transfer to a greased plate to cool, then chop and set aside.

Cook macaroni to al dente according to package directions; drain and set aside. Melt the butter in a saucepan over medium-high heat; whisk in the flour until blended. Whisk in the reduced bourbon and the remaining 1 tablespoon bourbon until smooth. Slowly whisk in the milk; cook until it thickens, stirring often. Whisk in the cheddar and provolone *(a handful at a time)*, paprika, salt, and black pepper until cheese melts. Pour over macaroni and add the bacon.

SERVES A CROWD

OKTOBERFEST CHEESE DIP

- 3 T. unsalted butter
- 3 T. flour
- ¾ C. **pumpkin ale**
- ¾ C. apple juice
- ¾ C. pumpkin purée
- 2 T. Dijon mustard
- ½ tsp. each pumpkin pie spice, garlic powder, cayenne pepper, and salt

- 6 oz. cream cheese, cubed
- 3½ C. shredded sharp cheddar cheese
- 4 bacon strips, cooked & crumbled
- 2 T. chopped chives
- Tortilla chips for serving

Beer

Grab a big saucepan and toss in the butter; let it melt over medium heat. Whisk in the flour and cook for 2 minutes. Add the pumpkin ale, juice, purée, and mustard, whisking to blend. Bring to a simmer and heat for 5 minutes or until thickened.

Stir in the pie spice, garlic powder, cayenne, and salt. Add the cream cheese and stir until melted. Add the cheddar *(½ cup at a time)*, making sure each addition is completely melted before adding the next. Carefully take a little taste and adjust the seasonings.

Transfer the dip to a serving bowl or small slow cooker set on low to keep warm; sprinkle with the bacon and chives. Serve immediately with tortilla chips. Yummm...

YES, IT'S FULL OF THE FLAVORS OF FALL, BUT YOU DON'T HAVE TO WAIT UNTIL OCTOBER TO TRY THIS DIP — IT'LL BE A HIT ANY TIME OF YEAR!

Peach Moon

*Pour ½ (12 oz.) bottle **orange-flavored beer** (like Blue Moon) into a tall glass. Add 1½ oz. (3 T.) peach schnapps and a generous ⅓ C. orange juice. Fill the glass with the rest of the beer and stir gently (don't get overzealous or the foam will explode out of the glass — seriously). Garnish with an orange slice.* **serves 2**

MAKES ABOUT 36

BOURBON BALLS

Stir together 3 C. vanilla wafer crumbs, 1 C. finely ground pecans, 1 C. powdered sugar, and 1½ T. unsweetened cocoa powder. Add 3 T. light corn syrup and ½ C. **bourbon** and stir well. Form into 1¼" balls and roll in powdered sugar, sugar, or crushed pecans. Set aside for an hour and roll again if using sugars. Store these babies tightly covered in the fridge.

MAKES 30

TIPSY FRIED PICKLES

Line a pan with foil and set a cooling rack over it. Beat 1 egg in a medium bowl until frothy. Stir in 1 tsp. baking soda, 1 tsp. paprika, 1 C. flour, and salt and black pepper to taste. Gradually add ¾ C. plus 2 T. **beer** *(we used lager)*; whisk until the batter is smooth. Put ¼ cup flour in a zippered plastic bag, add a few zesty dill pickle spears *(drained & patted dry)*, zip to close, and shake until coated; remove the pickles. Repeat until you've coated 30 pickles.

Heat 2" of canola oil to 350° in a deep-fryer or heavy saucepan. Coat a few pickles in batter and carefully set them in the hot oil. Fry until brown on all sides and transfer to the cooling rack. Repeat with the remaining pickles. Serve with ranch dressing for dipping.

MAKES 4 CUPS

HAPPY TIMES CORN CHOWDER

¼ C. unsalted butter

1 onion, diced

2 (14.75 oz.) cans creamed corn

½ tsp. ground nutmeg

1 to 1½ tsp. salt

Black pepper to taste

Several dashes of hot sauce

½ C. chicken stock

½ C. heavy cream

¼ C. **bourbon**

8 bacon strips, diced & cooked

Melt the butter in a saucepan over medium heat. Add the onion and cook for 5 minutes, until it starts to brown, stirring occasionally. Stir in the corn, nutmeg, salt, black pepper, hot sauce, stock, and cream. Let it simmer until it's piping hot, stirring occasionally.

Remove the saucepan from the heat and slowly stir in the bourbon. Ladle into mugs and top with a handful of bacon. Unbelievably wonderful!

Beer-Dipped Grilled Cheese

In a shallow bowl, whisk together 2 eggs, 1 C. **beer** *(we used brown ale)*, 2 T. flour, ½ tsp. salt, and ¼ tsp. chili powder. Cut 1 loaf of sourdough bread into eight slices, about ½" thick. Dunk both sides of one slice into the egg mixture, letting it set for a few seconds. Lift, let the excess drip back into the bowl, and set the bread slice on a tray. Top with a couple slices each of sharp cheddar cheese and cooked bacon. Dunk a second slice of bread and set on top. Repeat with the remaining bread, cheese, and bacon. Melt 2 T. butter in a griddle over medium heat. Set the sandwiches in the hot pan and cook until they're golden brown, then flip them over. When the other side is crispy and golden brown, remove from the heat and serve. Ooey, gooey goodness! *makes 4*

MAKES 12

SMOKY PECAN PIE BROWNIES

- 18 whole graham cracker rectangles
- 2 T. plus 1 C. brown sugar, divided
- 1¼ C melted butter, divided
- 2 C. sugar
- 1½ C. unsweetened cocoa powder
- 2 tsp. sea salt, divided
- ¾ C. plus 2 T. **beer**, divided (*we used coffee stout*)
- 1 tsp. plus 1 T. vanilla, divided
- 4 eggs plus 2 egg yolks, divided
- ⅔ C. flour
- ¾ tsp. smoked paprika
- ½ C. light corn syrup
- ¼ C. heavy cream
- 2 C. coarsely chopped pecans

Preheat the oven to 350°. Crush the graham crackers and mix with 2 tablespoons of the brown sugar and ½ cup butter. Press the mixture evenly into the bottom of a 9 x 13" baking pan and set aside.

In a bowl, stir together the sugar, cocoa powder, 1 teaspoon sea salt, ½ cup butter, ¾ cup beer, and 1 teaspoon vanilla. Add 2 of the eggs and the 2 egg yolks and stir to combine. Stir in the flour and paprika and then spread the mixture evenly over the crust. Bake for 20 minutes; remove from the oven and cool for 20 minutes. Reduce the oven temperature to 325°.

Grab a clean bowl and mix the remaining 1 cup brown sugar, ¼ cup butter, 2 tablespoons beer, and 2 eggs; stir in the syrup, cream, and pecans. Pour this evenly over the partially baked brownie layer, sprinkle with the remaining 1 teaspoon sea salt, and bake 40 to 50 minutes longer. The center will still be a little bit jiggly. Cool to room temperature, cover, and chill until set.

PURELY DECADENT! PURELY DELIGHTFUL.

Bourbon-Spiked Cupcakes

*Prepare 1 (15.25 oz.) pkg. French vanilla cake mix with eggs, oil, and water as directed on package, but replace ¼ of the water with **bourbon**. Divide the batter among 24 lined muffin cups and bake until cupcakes test done; cool. For frosting, beat 1 C. softened butter until creamy. Gradually add 7½ C. powdered sugar, ⅓ C. **bourbon**, and ⅓ C. whole milk until blended; stir in 1 T. vanilla. Frost cupcakes. **makes 24***

SERVES 4

IRRESISTIBLE BOURBON SALMON

¾ C. **bourbon**

⅔ C. brown sugar

1 tsp. minced garlic

1 tsp. apple cider vinegar

1 T. Worcestershire sauce

1 lb. salmon, patted dry

1 T. coarse sea salt

1½ tsp. black pepper

In a small saucepan, whisk together the bourbon, brown sugar, garlic, vinegar, and Worcestershire sauce, and bring it to a boil over high heat. Reduce the heat and let the glaze simmer about 10 minutes or until it is reduced to about half. Transfer to a little bowl and set it aside for now.

Preheat the broiler and line a baking sheet with buttered foil; set aside. Season both sides of salmon with sea salt and black pepper, and set on the prepped pan. Broil 4" from the heat for 8 minutes, until cooked through.

Immediately brush the salmon with some of the glaze. There are no rules – use as much or as little as you'd like. Once you take a taste, you might find yourself eating the glaze right out of the bowl. No rules, remember?

Butter-Beer Green Beans

Cook, drain, and crumble 6 bacon strips; set aside. In a saucepan, combine 1 (16 oz.) pkg. frozen cut green beans, ⅓ C. **beer** (we used light lager), and ⅓ C. butter (cut into small pieces); bring to a boil over medium heat. Reduce the heat to low, cover, and simmer for 6 to 8 minutes or until crisp-tender. Remove the beans with a slotted spoon, keeping the liquid in the saucepan. To the saucepan, add 3 T. brown sugar, 3 T. distilled white vinegar, 4 tsp. cornstarch, and 2 tsp. finely chopped white onion; stir until well blended. Bring to a boil and cook for a minute or two, until thickened. Stir in the beans and heat through. Sprinkle with set-aside bacon. **serves 4**

CROCKED CLUCKER TACOS

1 T. chili powder

1½ tsp. ground cumin

½ tsp. smoked paprika

Pinch of cayenne pepper

1½ tsp. salt

½ tsp. black pepper

1 (12 oz.) bottle **beer**, divided *(we used wheat ale)*

3½ lbs. chicken breast meat

1 (16 oz.) jar thick black bean and corn salsa

Chopped fresh cilantro to taste

1 small chopped onion

A handful of grape tomatoes, diced

24 (6") corn tortillas

Vegetable oil for frying

Your favorite toppings

Mix chili powder, cumin, paprika, cayenne, salt, and black pepper; pull out 1½ tablespoons and set it aside. To the remainder, stir in ¾ cup beer.

Put the chicken in a greased slow cooker and pour in the spicy beer mixture. Cook on low 6 to 8 hours *(high, 3 to 4 hours)*, until done *(don't over-cook)*. Meanwhile, stir together the salsa, cilantro, onion, tomatoes, and as much of the remaining ½ cup of beer as you'd like without thinning the salsa too much; refrigerate until you're ready to use it.

When the chicken is done, uncover the cooker, but don't turn it off. Shred the meat and let it soak in the juices about 20 minutes. Meanwhile, fry the tortillas one at a time in hot oil until crisp, folding slightly into a taco shell shape; drain on paper towels.

Taste the chicken and stir in more of the set-aside spice mixture if you'd like. Pile the meat, chilled salsa, and your favorite toppings into the shells. They're beer-y, beer-y good!

Bourbon

SERVES 12

SLOW COOKER
BOURBON STREET CHICKEN

2 T. cornstarch

2 T. olive oil

2 tsp. minced garlic

¼ tsp. each ground ginger,
   salt, and cayenne pepper

2 T. applesauce

¼ C. **bourbon**

⅓ C. brown sugar

2 T. ketchup

1 T. apple cider vinegar

½ C. water

⅓ C. soy sauce

3 lbs. chicken breast meat,
   cut into bite-size pieces

4 bacon strips, cooked
   & crumbled

Cooked rice

1 fresh pineapple, peeled
   & cut into bite-size
   pieces

In a 3-quart slow cooker, combine the cornstarch, oil, garlic, ginger, salt, cayenne, applesauce, bourbon, brown sugar, ketchup, vinegar, water, and soy sauce; whisk together until nicely blended.

Toss the chicken pieces into the cooker, add the bacon, and give it a good stir – you want the chicken pieces evenly coated. Are they coated? If so, cover the cooker, set it to low, and walk away for 4 hours or until the chicken is done *(in the meantime, grab a cold beer from the fridge or go enjoy happy hour at your favorite pub)*.

When you come back, you'll be greeted with an aroma that is out of this world.

Put rice on serving plates, top with the chicken and sauce from the cooker, and toss on some pineapple pieces. Go ahead – pile it all on!

Bourbon Peach Slush

*Dump 1 (16 oz.) pkg. frozen peaches (about 3 C.) into a blender container along with 1 C. chilled ginger ale, 4 oz. (½ C.) **bourbon** (more or less to taste), 2 T. sugar (more or less to taste), and the juice of 1 lime. Process until relatively smooth. Pour into two big glasses. Slurp, let the brain freeze subside, and slurp some more.* **makes 2 big servings**

SERVES 8

FRENCH DIP SANDWICHES

Preheat the oven to 350°. Set a 4 lb. beef rump roast *(trimmed)* into a big slow cooker. Add 1 (10.5 oz.) can beef broth, 1 (10.5 oz.) can French onion soup, and 1 (12 oz.) bottle **beer** *(we used x-tra stout)*. Cover and cook on low 7 to 8 hours *(high, 3½ to 4 hours)*.

Split a loaf of French bread lengthwise and spread cut sides with butter; cut into sandwich-size pieces. Bake butter side up 10 to 15 minutes, until heated through and lightly toasted. Meanwhile, cut the meat into thin slices. Pile meat and provolone cheese slices on the bottoms of the sandwiches; bake a few minutes to melt the cheese. Replace the tops and serve with the juice from the cooker.

Bourbon

SERVES 4

DRUNKEN PULLED PORK PIZZA

Preheat the oven to 400° and preheat a pizza pan. While the oven is heating, warm 4 to 5 C. of the meat and onions from **Drunken Pulled Pork** *(page 52)*.

Set 1 (12") precooked pizza crust *(like Mama Mary's)* on the hot pan and brush 1 T. olive oil and 1 T. **bourbon** over the top of the entire crust; spread with some BBQ sauce *(try the Bourbon 'Q' Sauce from page 53)* to within ½" of the edge and top with the warm pork and onions. Add mushrooms and jalapeños or any other toppings to taste. Cover with as much shredded Pepper Jack cheese as you'd like.

Bake 10 to 15 minutes or until the cheese is melted. Serve with extra BBQ sauce. Now THAT'S a great pizza!

SERVES 6

BEER-BATTERED COD

Vegetable oil for frying

6 to 8 (6 oz.) cod fillets, patted dry

6 ciabatta or potato rolls

2 T. Old Bay seafood seasoning

1 C. flour

2 tsp. each garlic salt and black pepper

1 (12 oz.) bottle **beer** *(we used lager)*

1 egg, beaten

Tartar sauce and coleslaw for serving, optional

Preheat the oven to 275° and set a baking sheet in the oven. Heat oil in a deep-fryer to 365°. Meanwhile, cut the fish to fit the rolls.

In a bowl, mix Old Bay, flour, garlic salt, and black pepper. In a separate bowl, whisk together the beer and egg; add to the dry ingredients and stir to combine. One or two at a time, dip the fish into the batter, letting the excess drip off, and carefully add to the hot oil. Fry for 5 to 7 minutes, until golden brown on the outside and opaque in the middle. Set the fried fish on the hot baking sheet in the oven to keep warm. Repeat with the remaining fish. Serve on rolls with tartar sauce and slaw.

Oven Beer Fries

Cut 1½ lbs. russet potatoes into ½"-thick slices; cut the slices into big french fry shapes. In a big bowl, mix 1 (12 oz.) bottle **beer** *(we used pale ale)* and 1 T. sea salt; add the potatoes and enough water to submerge. Cover and chill 3 hours. Position an oven rack in the top ⅓ of the oven and preheat the oven to 425°. Drain the potatoes, rinse, pat dry, and dump into a clean bowl. Add ¼ C. canola oil and 1 tsp. each sea salt, garlic powder, onion powder, and paprika, and ½ tsp. each black pepper and sugar. Toss to coat the potatoes and spread them out on a rimmed baking sheet. Bake for 20 minutes, flip, and bake 20 minutes longer or until a delicious deep golden brown. ***serves 4 to 6***

*Pssst...once these fries are baked, they can be dipped in any leftover batter from the **Beer-Battered Cod** and then fried to crispy perfection.*

SERVES 18

SLOSHED APPLE CAKE

4 C. peeled, coarsely chopped baking apples *(we used Pink Lady and Granny Smith)*

¾ C. coarsely chopped walnuts

1 C. plus 2 tsp. **bourbon**, divided

½ C. vegetable oil

2 eggs, beaten

2¼ C. sugar, divided

2 C. flour

2 tsp. each baking soda and cinnamon

1 tsp. each salt and ground nutmeg

¼ tsp. ground cloves

2 C. whipping cream

Soak the apples and walnuts in 1 cup bourbon for 1 hour, stirring occasionally.

After an hour, preheat the oven to 350° and grease a 9 x 13" baking pan.

In a big bowl, stir together the oil, eggs, and 2 cups of the sugar. In a separate bowl, mix the flour, baking soda, cinnamon, salt, nutmeg, and cloves. Add the dry ingredients to the wet ingredients and stir to combine. Dump the apples and walnuts along with the soaking liquid into the batter, stirring to blend. Transfer the batter to the prepped pan and bake for 45 to 50 minutes or until the cake tests done.

While the cake cools, pour the whipping cream into a chilled bowl and beat on high speed using chilled beaters, gradually beating in the remaining ¼ cup sugar and 2 teaspoons bourbon until stiff peaks form. Serve with the cake.

Chocolate-Guinness Float

*Place two scoops of chocolate ice cream in a mug. Fill with chilled **beer** (we used x-tra stout, but you could also try a chocolate stout). That's it! Simple and delicious!* **makes 1**

*Try a Bourbon-Ginger Beer Float: 2 scoops of vanilla ice cream and 2 oz. **bourbon** topped off with chilled ginger beer.* **makes 1**

STOUT FRENCH ONION SOUP

About 6 medium
   yellow onions

3 tsp. minced garlic

2 T. butter

1 (8 oz.) pkg. sliced baby
   Portobello mushrooms

6 C. beef broth

½ C. **stout beer**

1 T. soy sauce

1 tsp. red wine vinegar

¼ tsp. each dried
   rosemary and thyme

Salt & black pepper
   to taste

Sourdough or French bread

6 oz. Irish cheddar cheese,
   sliced

Get out a sharp knife, a cutting board, and plenty of tissues. You're slicing onions, and lots of 'em. Slice 'em nice and thin, until you get 8 cups.

Dump the sliced onions, garlic, butter, and mushrooms into a big slow cooker. Cover and cook on high for 1 hour or until the onions begin to soften. Add the broth, beer, soy sauce, vinegar, rosemary, thyme, salt, and black pepper and stir to combine. Cover and cook on low for 6 to 8 hours (high, 3 to 4 hours), until the onions are nice and tender.

Just before serving, preheat the broiler. Cut the bread into pieces that will fit in your serving bowls and top with the cheese. Broil a minute or two until the cheese is bubbly and slightly browned, watching carefully so it doesn't burn.

Ladle the soup into bowls and top with the toasted cheese bread. So good it's worth all those tears!

MAKES 1½ QUARTS

NO-CHURN DELUXE ICE CREAM

Melt 2 T. butter in a big skillet over medium-high heat. Add 4 C. fresh or frozen pitted tart cherries and 2 T. brown sugar and bring to a boil. Boil for several minutes, until the liquid reduces to just a few tablespoons. Take the skillet off the heat and stir in 2 T. **bourbon**. Set aside until cool.

In a chilled mixing bowl, combine 2 C. heavy cream, 1 (14 oz.) can sweetened condensed milk, and the seeds from 1 vanilla bean *(or use 1 tsp. vanilla instead)*. Beat until stiff peaks form. Carefully stir in 1 C. mini chocolate chips along with the cooled cherries and every delicious drop of their liquid. Transfer the mixture to a lidded freezer-safe container and freeze at least 4 hours. Simply incredible!

SERVES 4

BERRY BOURBON LEMONADE

Make a simple syrup by combining ¼ C. sugar, ¼ C. brown sugar, and ½ C. water in a saucepan; bring to a simmer over medium heat, stirring until the sugars dissolve. Set this syrup aside to cool.

Juice 2 lemons and set the juice aside *(you'll need about ½ C.)*. With a vegetable peeler, peel off thin strips of the lemon rind, avoiding the white pith, and toss into a pitcher along with 2 C. fresh blackberries and 12 fresh mint leaves. Muddle together until you get some nice juice from the berries. Pour in 4 oz. *(½ C. or more to taste)* **bourbon**, set-aside lemon juice, and cooled simple syrup; give it a little stir to combine. Divide the bourbon mixture among four ice-filled glasses, pouring through a strainer to remove pulp. Garnish with extra blackberries, lemon slices, and mint leaves.

SERVES 12

DRUNKEN PULLED PORK

1½ tsp. paprika

1 tsp. each onion powder and garlic powder

1 tsp. each dried oregano and thyme

½ tsp. black pepper

Salt

3½ lbs. boneless pork roast

2 T. vegetable oil

2 T. butter

2 onions, sliced

1 (12 oz.) bottle **beer**, divided *(we used India pale ale)*

¾ C. BBQ sauce, your favorite *(Bourbon 'Q' Sauce, next page, tastes great here)*

Buns

Stir together the paprika, onion powder, garlic powder, oregano, thyme, black pepper, and 1 teaspoon salt. Rub this mixture evenly over the pork. Yes, you can use your hands.

Heat the oil in a skillet over medium-high heat and add the pork, turning to brown all sides. When it's nice and brown, put it in a greased 3-quart slow cooker. Put the butter in the hot skillet and add the onions, a pinch of salt, and half the beer *(set the remaining beer aside)*; cook about 10 minutes, until tender, then dump the onions and the juices over the pork. Mix the BBQ sauce with the set-aside beer and pour it over the onions. Set the cooker to low and let it do its thing for 8 hours *(high, 4 hours)* or until the pork is done.

Once the pork is cooked to perfection, pull it out of the cooker and set it on a rimmed baking pan to contain the mess. Shred the meat and serve on buns. Yes, you can add cabbage and extra **Bourbon 'Q' Sauce**! Yes, you're gonna love it!

Note: Use leftovers for **Drunken Pulled Pork Pizza** *(page 43)*.

Bourbon 'Q' Sauce

In a saucepan, mix 1 C. ketchup, ½ C. **bourbon**, 3 T. brown sugar, 3 T. molasses, 3 T. apple cider vinegar, 2 T. Worcestershire sauce, 1 T. soy sauce, 1 T. Dijon mustard, 1½ tsp. liquid smoke, 1 tsp. each onion powder and garlic powder, and ½ tsp. each crushed red pepper and black pepper; bring to a boil, stirring occasionally. Reduce heat and simmer until reduced to 2 cups, stirring often. Use in **Drunken Pulled Pork** on previous page and anywhere else you please.

SERVES 4

PALE ALE & CHILI-LIME DRUMETTES

1 (12 oz.) bottle **beer** *(we used white ale)*

3 T. tomato paste

3 T. lime juice

1 T. chili powder

½ tsp. each salt, smoked paprika, and garlic powder

2 T. honey

1 T. soy sauce

2 tsp. hot sauce

2 lbs. chicken drumettes

Pour the beer into a big bowl. Whisk in the tomato paste, lime juice, chili powder, salt, paprika, garlic powder, honey, soy sauce, and hot sauce until well blended and smooth. Transfer to a big zippered plastic bag; add the drumettes, zip to close, turn to coat, and refrigerate several hours.

After the drumettes have marinated several hours, position an oven rack in the top ⅓ of the oven and preheat the oven to 400°. Pour the marinade from the bag into a saucepan. Bring to a boil over high heat and cook for 20 minutes or until thickened and reduced, stirring often.

Line a rimmed baking sheet with foil and coat with cooking spray. Dip the drumettes into the thickened sauce and arrange them on the baking sheet. Bake for 10 minutes, brush with more sauce, and flip. Repeat every 10 minutes for 40 minutes until cooked through.

If you'd like, pop the pan of drumettes under the broiler for a minute or two to crisp up after you take them out of the oven.

Beer

Lemon Shandy

*Rim four tall glasses with lemon juice and coarse sugar. Fill the glasses with ice and pour ½ C. lemonade into each. Top off each glass with ½ C. of your favorite **beer** (we used light beer). Garnish with a lemon slice.* **serves 4**

Bourbon & Beer

MAKES 8

BEER & BOURBON KABOBS

½ C. **beer** *(we used oatmeal stout)*

¼ C. **bourbon**

¼ C. soy sauce

2 T. coarse grain mustard

3 T. brown sugar

½ tsp. salt

2 tsp. coarse black pepper

½ tsp. Worcestershire sauce

¼ C. minced green onions

1 lb. chicken breast meat, cut into 1" chunks

1 (8 oz.) pkg. whole mushrooms

2 bell peppers, any color, cut into 1" chunks

1 yellow onion, cut into 1" chunks

Cooked rice for serving

Combine the beer, bourbon, soy sauce, mustard, sugar, salt, black pepper, Worcestershire sauce, and green onions in a big zippered plastic bag; zip to close and rub between your hands to blend ingredients. Add the chicken, zip closed, and chill for several hours, turning occasionally.

Preheat the oven to 450° and place the oven rack in the top position. Line a baking sheet with foil and coat the foil with cooking spray. Thread the mushrooms, chicken, bell peppers, and onion onto metal skewers. Set the skewers on the prepped baking sheet and brush with some of the marinade *(go ahead – give them a good soaking)*; bake for 15 minutes or until the chicken is done.

Keeping in mind that the skewers are now scorching hot, grab them using an oven mitt and put on plates with rice. Serve piping hot.

Beernana Bread

Preheat the oven to 375° and grease a 5 x 9" loaf pan. In a bowl, mix 3 C. self-rising flour, ¾ C. quick-cooking oats, and ½ C. brown sugar. In a separate bowl, stir together 1½ C. mashed ripe bananas, ¼ C. pure maple syrup, and 1 (12 oz.) bottle **beer** *(we used a Bavarian-style wheat, but you could also try a banana or banana bread beer)*. Stir the flour mixture into the banana mixture until just moistened. Spread evenly in the prepped pan and sprinkle with 1 T. sesame seed and ¼ tsp. coarse salt. Bake 55 to 60 minutes or until the bread tests done. Cool in pan 10 minutes before removing to a cooling rack. Delicious toasted! ***makes 1 loaf***

MAKES 6

HOPS & ZEST 'CAKES WITH BOOZED-UP SYRUP

- 1½ C. brown sugar
- ½ C. **beer** *(we used light lager)*
- Butter
- 1 tsp. cinnamon, divided
- 2 eggs, room temperature
- ½ tsp. cream of tartar
- ½ C. **beer** *(we used wheat ale)*
- ¼ C. buttermilk
- 1 tsp. vanilla
- 1 T. orange zest
- 1 C. flour
- 3 T. sugar
- 1 tsp. baking powder
- ½ tsp. each baking soda and salt

For the syrup, put the brown sugar, light beer, 3 tablespoons butter, and ½ teaspoon cinnamon in a small saucepan over medium-low heat until it just begins to boil, stirring to dissolve; keep warm.

For the pancakes, separate the egg whites and yolks into two bowls. Add the cream of tartar to the whites and beat on high speed until stiff peaks form. To the yolks, add the wheat ale, buttermilk, vanilla, and zest, and beat until well mixed. In a big bowl, stir together the flour, sugar, baking powder, baking soda, salt, and the remaining ½ teaspoon cinnamon. Add the yolk mixture to the dry ingredients and stir until combined. Gently fold in the egg whites until batter is blended.

Using about ½ cup for each pancake, pour batter onto a hot nonstick griddle or skillet. Cook until bubbles form around the edges; flip and cook until golden brown on the other side. Serve with butter and warm syrup.

Bourbon

Boozy Cherries

*In a small saucepan over low heat, simmer ¾ C. **bourbon** with 2½ T. sugar until sugar dissolves; remove from the heat and let stand 15 minutes. Pack 1 C. frozen (thawed) sweet cherries in a lidded glass jar and pour syrup over the fruit to cover. Cover tightly and store in the refrigerator. Serve over cake or ice cream or in beverages for a sweet little kick.*
makes 1 cup

SERVES A CROWD

FIRECRACKER CHEESE SPREAD

In a food processor, combine 8 oz. shredded smoked sharp cheddar cheese, 8 oz. shredded apple-smoked white cheddar cheese, 3 T. **bourbon**, ¼ C. pickled jalapeños and their juice, 1 tsp. salt, and ⅓ C. plus 2 tsp. **beer** *(we used oatmeal stout)* until everything is well blended and a spreading consistency; transfer to a bowl.

Serve with party rye bread, crackers *(a roasted garlic kind tastes great)*, and veggies.

Bourbon

SERVES 4

DOUSED & SOUSED WINGS

Put 2½ lbs. chicken wings in a big zippered plastic bag. Whisk together 3 to 4 T. Dijon mustard, 2 C. **bourbon**, 2 T. angostura bitters, and ¾ C. sugar and pour into the bag with the wings. Zip to close and toss it into the fridge for several hours or overnight to marinate.

When you're ready to bake the wings, preheat the oven to 400°. Arrange the wings on a foil-lined and greased rimmed baking sheet and pour the marinade into a saucepan. Bake the wings for 35 to 40 minutes or until cooked through, brushing with marinade a couple of times during baking. In the meantime, boil the marinade until reduced by half. Serve the sauce with the wings and get out the napkins!

Index

Desserts

BARREL OF FUN

Bourbon can't be aged in just any old barrel. The distilled clear liquor *("white dog")* must go into a brand new oak barrel – never a used one – that's been charred inside. Then it soaks at least two years to pick up just the right natural caramel color and smoky flavor.

If a batch of bourbon comes from one barrel – and only one – before being filtered, mixed with water, and bottled, it's a "single-barrel bourbon." Its flavor is unique to that particular barrel *(and it's probably pricey)*. But big distillers mix many different barrels of bourbon together to get the consistent flavor they want. This means your favorite brand will taste the same every time you buy it.

Bourbon-licious

All bourbon is whiskey, but not all whiskey is bourbon.

Official bourbon is only made in the USA and has at least 51% corn along with water, other grains, and yeast. Whiskeys like Scotch, Irish, and Tennessee can be distilled elsewhere, have added flavorings and colorings, and be aged or filtered differently.

Bourbon Hand-Me-Downs

What happens to the old bourbon barrels? They're reused to age other whiskeys and some dark beers. Barrel-aged beers pick up a natural flavor from those barrels that can't quite be copied by tossing toasted oak chips into steel barrels. But beer ages to perfection much faster than bourbon.

A Toast to Bourbon & Beer!